Essential Question
What kinds of stories do we tell?
Why do we tell them?

PAUL BUNYAN

BY MAY KENNEDY
ILLUSTRATED BY ALVARO FERNANDEZ VILLA

CHAPTER 1

THE GIANT BABY

Long ago in the state of Maine, a giant baby boy was born. When the baby was only two weeks old, he was as large as an adult. And he had a gigantic, black, bushy beard!

The baby's name was Paul Bunyan. He grew and grew. By the time he was just nine months old, he was 10 feet tall! He had to wear the clothes of an extremely large man. He wore blue jeans, a red plaid shirt, and huge leather boots.

When baby Paul Bunyan started to crawl, it was as if an earthquake had struck. The ground shook, the buildings in the village wobbled, and the trees in the forest rocked from side to side.

The shaking ground frightened the townsfolk. They crouched inside doorways and dived under tables, staying like that until the shaking subsided. Of course, the shaking hardly ever stopped. Babies like to explore their surroundings, and Paul Bunyan was no exception.

The unhappy townsfolk demanded that Paul Bunyan's parents do something about their baby. His parents reluctantly placed their beloved boy in a huge, floating cradle and then pushed the cradle off the coast of Maine. "Farewell!" called Paul Bunyan's mother, crying as she waved good-bye.

However, the situation soon grew worse. When baby Paul turned in his cradle, gigantic waves crashed along the beaches and flooded entire towns. Then the cradle washed back to shore.

Paul Bunyan's parents were desperate. They took baby Paul deep into the Maine woods and left him in the safety of a cave far away from civilization. They did not want to abandon their son, but they had no alternative.

Paul Bunyan's father gave his son a knife, an ax, a fishing pole, and some flint rocks to help him survive in the wilderness. His mother tried to be brave as she said farewell to her precious son.

Baby Paul was heartbroken. He wept so much that a river of tears formed at his feet.

One day, as he cried into the winding river, he heard a splash. "It's a trout!" he exclaimed. He quickly grabbed his fishing pole and captured the trout. He used his knife to clean the fish. Then he used his ax to chop firewood and the flint rocks to start a fire. Soon Paul was eating a delicious meal, and his heavy heart felt much lighter.

STOP AND CHECK

Why did Paul Bunyan's parents leave him in the woods?

CHAPTER 2

A WORLD OF BLUE

Now Paul Bunyan knew that he could live comfortably in the Maine woods. He could take care of himself by fishing and hunting for food. Trees were plentiful in the enormous woods, so there was always lumber for making fires, which allowed him to cook and to keep warm.

Paul Bunyan lived alone for the next 20 years. He had to be very brave. He had to battle against the harsh seasons to survive. The winters were extreme, with ferocious snowstorms and blizzards. There were many floods in the spring. He had to fight forest fires, which were lit by lightning during the summer thunderstorms. He had to wrestle the wild, whipping winds of fall.

On one particularly cold winter's day, Paul Bunyan's life changed forever. Great gusts of snow flew into the entrance of his cave, but the snow was not white. it was blue!

Paul Bunyan had never seen anything like it. He peered out of his cave. The blue snow had blanketed the trees and land as far as he could see.

"It is absolutely beautiful!" he exclaimed. "It is the color of a magnificent, blue lake."

Paul Bunyan was extremely curious. Dressed in his warmest clothes and boots, he sauntered across the blue, snow-covered land. Lightning zapped and thunder clapped in the wintry skies above him.

Suddenly a wild, westerly wind whistled past Paul Bunyan. The wind and the thunder were so deafening that they almost drowned out a faint "maa-maa" sound. Paul Bunyan looked around. He tried to find out what was making the noise. All he could hear was the thunder and wind. Then he noticed a tail poking out of the blue snow.

He pulled and pulled on the tail. Finally, out popped the biggest baby ox on Earth—and that is no exaggeration! The baby ox was blue like the surrounding snow, but its horns were the color of delicate, white snowflakes.

Paul Bunyan crouched on the icy ground beside the baby ox. He gently scooped up the ox in his cradling arms and carried it back to his cave.

Once inside, he carefully placed the baby ox on the ground. He put more wood on the crackling fire to thaw the frozen animal. "You will be safe here in my cozy cave," Paul told the frightened creature. Curled up by the fire, the ox looked like a sleeping child posed for a painting.

By morning, the ox was stronger and happier. At last, Paul Bunyan had a friend. He named his friend Babe the Blue Ox.

Babe was much like Paul in that he grew very rapidly. When Babe was a full-grown ox, he was the staggering height of 42 ax handles. Babe's hunger and thirst became greater as he grew bigger, and this was a problem. Paul needed a watering hole big enough for Babe's thirst, so he took a few giant strides west and dug gigantic ponds in the ground. Today we call Babe's enormous watering holes the Great Lakes.

STOP AND CHECK

How did Paul Bunyan find his new friend?

CHAPTER 3

THE GIANT LUMBERJACK

Paul Bunyan and Babe enjoyed wandering through the woods and admiring the trees. Paul Bunyan knew, though, that people needed these trees to build homes, barns, and wagons. So he picked up his ax and gave it a mighty swing. In the blink of an eye, ten white pines plunged to the forest floor. Then, one after another, he brought more impressive pines crashing down.

Babe looked puzzled. "We must get this lumber to a sawmill," explained Paul Bunyan to his friend.

The giant lumberjack stacked the trees onto Babe's colossal back. The closest sawmill was by the Big Onion River in Minnesota. Paul and Babe left Maine. They commenced their journey, taking the most enormous steps that you can imagine.

Along the way, Paul Bunyan saw a river and thought that the logs would travel well on it. But with all the twists and turns in the river, he knew that the logs would jam along their watery route.

"You can help straighten this river," said Paul Bunyan to Babe. "All you have to do is pull."

Paul Bunyan tied two ropes to Babe's harness and their other ends to the opposite side of the twisting river. Then he asked Babe to pull. Soon the river was as straight as a tree trunk. Finally, the two friends could float hundreds of logs down the river to the sawmill.

Paul Bunyan and Babe worked tirelessly. They floated log after log down the river. It was exhausting work, even for a giant lumberjack and his equally giant helper. After a day of hard work, Paul would wring out his clothes, and a great waterfall of perspiration would fall to the ground.

One night while resting under the stars, Paul Bunyan came up with an idea. "We need help," he explained to Babe. "We need loggers to come and work for us. They can share our heavy workload. I think it is time we started a logging camp."

With that, Paul Bunyan made giant-sized signs advertising that he needed workers to help him in his logging camp. He hammered the signs into the ground for miles around. Soon hundreds of thousands of workers applied for the positions. Paul Bunyan knew the kind of people that he needed. They should be more than 10 feet tall and be able to pop six buttons off their shirts with one breath! Amazingly, more than a thousand workers met these requirements.

Soon Paul Bunyan built a logging camp. The bunkhouses were a mile long. The dining tables were so enormous that it took one whole week to pass food from one end to the other!

Paul Bunyan had another, far greater problem. The camp cook could not make food quickly enough to feed the thousand workers with their huge appetites. As always, Paul Bunyan had a solution. He built an ice-rink-sized griddle for the cook, and he lit a forest fire to heat it. However, the camp cook was still not satisfied. "How will I grease this gigantic pan?" he cried.

Once again, Paul Bunyan knew exactly what to do. He had a hundred men tie bacon fat to the soles of their shoes. Then they skated around the pan to grease it.

Every day, Paul Bunyan solved problems at the camp. When the workers suffered from frostbite, he suggested that they grow their beards. The men grew their whiskers down to their feet. Then they knitted their beards into socks!

Paul Bunyan had started out life alone in a gloomy cave. Now, many years later, thousands of workers in the logging camp looked up to this larger-than-life giant lumberjack. Yet Paul Bunyan never tried to impress anyone, and he never tried to be someone he was not.

Paul Bunyan and his faithful friend Babe helped many people during their lives. They cleared trees so that the farmers in Kansas and Iowa could plant wheat and corn.

For years and years, the loggers sat around the camp after a hard day working in the woods, telling stories about the heroic Paul Bunyan. They talked about all his good deeds and the good times they had shared with him and Babe.

The loggers also told a story of Paul Bunyan's journey through Arizona. As he walked, he dragged his pickax behind him. This created a large ditch. Today we call that ditch the Grand Canyon.

But the wilderness was always calling Paul Bunyan and Babe. They were last seen wandering toward the Arctic Circle. It seems a curious place for a lumberjack to want to go because trees do not grow in that vast, icy land. Maybe Paul Bunyan and Babe wanted to visit a frozen frontier where they could rest for a short while!

STOP AND CHECK

How did Paul Bunyan solve the cook's problems?

Respond to Reading

Summarize

Use important details from the story to summarize *Paul Bunyan*. Your graphic organizer may help you.

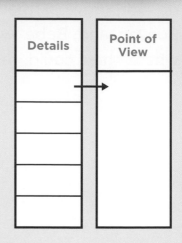

Details | Point of View

Text Evidence

1. How do you know that *Paul Bunyan* is a tall tale? Give details about the characters and events. **GENRE**

2. What does the narrator think of Paul Bunyan? Give an example of a description that shows this. **POINT OF VIEW**

3. What does the word *twisting* mean on page 11? Use context clues and an antonym in the paragraph to help you. **SYNONYMS AND ANTONYMS**

4. Write about the narrator's view of Babe. **WRITE ABOUT READING**

Compare Texts

Read a legend about a very clever girl.

One Grain of Rice

Long ago in India, there lived a *raja*, or ruler. This raja decided that all the rice farmers in the land should give him most of what they grew. He wanted to store rice away for times of famine. Before long, the royal storehouses were bursting with rice.

Then one year, the rice crops failed. The people were extremely hungry, but the raja would not give them any rice.

"I cannot go hungry," he said. "I must keep every grain of rice for myself."

The people grew hungrier and hungrier, but this did not worry the raja. One day, he even ordered a feast to be prepared in his palace.

A servant and an elephant were sent to fetch rice from a storehouse. As the elephant lumbered back to the palace, grains of rice overflowed from the baskets tied to its back. A village girl named Rani quickly ran beside the elephant and caught the rice with her skirt.

"Stop! Rice thief!" cried a palace guard.

Rani thought quickly. She pretended she had done a good deed for the raja. "I'm collecting the rice to return it to the raja," said Rani.

When the raja heard what had happened, he decided that Rani deserved a reward. Clever Rani asked for only one grain of rice.

"One grain of rice?" cried the raja. "Let me reward you with more than that."

"All right," said Rani. "You could give me one grain of rice today. Then each day for 30 days, you could double the number of grains of rice that you gave me the day before."

The raja thought that Rani's request was very reasonable. He handed Rani one grain of rice.

On the second day, Rani received two grains of rice. On the third day, she received four grains. On the thirteenth day, she was handed 4,096 grains of rice. By the thirtieth day, it took hundreds of elephants to transport all of Rani's rice. Through the process of doubling, one grain of rice had quickly turned into more than one billion grains of rice!

"Now I have no rice!" exclaimed the raja. "What will I do?"

Rani was a kind girl. She gave nearly all of her rice to the starving people, keeping only one basket of rice. Rani gave this rice to the raja—but only after he promised to take just the rice that he needed from that day forward. Of course, he agreed.

Make Connections

Why do you think people write legends like *One Grain of Rice*? ESSENTIAL QUESTION

How are Paul Bunyan and Rani similar? How are they different? TEXT TO TEXT

Focus on Genre

Tall Tales Tall tales are stories about people with amazing abilities that cannot be real. These tales often encourage qualities that are valued in a culture. Sometimes a tall tale is based on the life of a real person, but what he or she did is exaggerated.

Read and Find As Paul Bunyan grows, his exploits become more and more incredible. These are described using exaggerated comparisons. For example, when baby Paul crawled, "the buildings in the village wobbled." (page 2)

Your Turn

What abilities do you value? Work with a partner to list several of these abilities.

Choose two of these abilities. For each one, write an exaggerated comparison to describe a person who has this ability. For example, "She could dribble the ball around the moon and back again in the blink of an eye."

Illustrate one of your comparisons and share it with the class.